In Silence

poems by

Paulette Demers Turco

Finishing Line Press
Georgetown, Kentucky

In Silence

Copyright © 2018 by Paulette Demers Turco
ISBN 978-1-63534-529-2 First Edition
All rights reserved under International and Pan-American Copyright Conventions.
No part of this book may be reproduced in any manner whatsoever without written permission from the publisher, except in the case of brief quotations embodied in critical articles and reviews.

ACKNOWLEDGMENTS

The poems in this book have been influenced and improved by the inspiration, mentoring and encouragement of Paulette Demers Turco's poetry mentors, Rhina Espaillat, Alfred Nicol, and Deborah Warren, and by her workshop poetry friends.

Her loving family and people in her varied life experiences helped inspire these poems.

A pensive walk along the Plum Island shore, after a September, 2017 sunrise, inspired the cover photo, *Dawn on Plum Island*.

Special thanks are extended to: Priscilla Turner Spada, who assisted her in editing this manuscript and guiding her through the details of the submission process, and Greg Nikas Photography in Newburyport, MA, for the author photos, a fun experience.

"Work or Play" was first published in *The Lyric*, in Spring, 2016.

"Rushmore" was first published in *Ibbetson Street Press* November/December, 2016.

Earlier versions of "Mariposa Monarca," and "The Limpet" were published in *Merrimac Mic Anthology II: Going with the Floes*, Isabell VanMerlin, Editor, 2016.

"Rushmore" and "I Always Knew" were published with accompanying art in *Merrimac Mic Anthology III: the River Widens*, Isabell VanMerlin, Editor, 2017. The anthology gave acknowledgement to *Ibbetson Street Press* for its first publication of *Rushmore*.

"Birch, Ice, Snow" was first published in *Ibbetson Street Press*, November/December, 2017, and later in *Merrimac Mic Anthology IV: Watershed*, March 2018.

Publisher: Leah Maines
Editor: Christen Kincaid
Cover Art: Paulette Demers Turco
Author Photo: Greg Nikas Photography
Cover Design: Elizabeth Maines McCleavy

Printed in the USA on acid-free paper.
Order online: www.finishinglinepress.com
also available on amazon.com

Author inquiries and mail orders:
Finishing Line Press
P. O. Box 1626
Georgetown, Kentucky 40324
U. S. A.

Table of Contents

Seasons Triolets 1

I Always Knew 3

The Limpet 4

Birch, Ice, Snow 5

Float 6

Work or Play 7

Mother's Day 8

She Dreamed 9

Mariposa Monarca 10

Plunge 11

She Had To 12

Solace 13

Beneath His Bed 14

From Rubble 15

In Olneyville 16

Shimmer 17

Ribbons, Buttons, Lace 18

Rushmore 20

Hours Arrested 21

Lift 22

*To my dear parents,
Raymond and Dorothy,
to my dear sons,
Damian and Andrew,
and to my
dearest granddaughters,
Bianca and Charlotte*

Seasons Triolets

Float
Snowflakes float as if in flight
in silence as they spiral down—
crystals sparkling day or night.
Snowflakes float as if in flight
creating images in white
as children sled down hills in town.
Snowflakes float as if in flight
in silence as they spiral down.

Plunge
Raindrops plunge through glistening air;
in streaks of mist, they soak the ground
creating cloaks of haze and glare.
Raindrops plunge through glistening air
as tulips break through soil, once bare,
and children's boots splash puddled ground.
Raindrops plunge through glistening air;
in streaks of mist, they soak the ground.

Shimmer
Sun rays shimmer in the air.
Time melts as foam-topped waves crash down
on sparkling sand out to the pier.
Sun rays shimmer in the air.
At high tide, castles disappear.
A child's towel becomes a gown.
Sun rays shimmer in the air.
Time melts as foam-topped waves crash down.

Lift
Leaves lift free on chilling gusts
and rustle, whisper, swirl around—
orange, yellow, red, then rust.
Leaves lift free on chilling gusts
while children trick or treat with trust
and scarecrows, pumpkins dot the ground.
Leaves lift free on chilling gusts
and rustle, whisper, swirl around.

I Always Knew

Reflection on Narihira's LVI

*I have always known
That at last I would
Take this road, but yesterday
I did not know that it would be today.*

I always knew
I would take the road away.
I didn't know—why.

I always knew
I would take the road away.
I needed—to learn.

I always knew
I would take the road away.
I didn't know—alone.

I always knew
I would take the road away.
I didn't know…

I didn't know
the silent fears
I felt at home
would follow me.

The Limpet

The Limpet's tendrils grip its conical shell
against percussive waves on a granite cliff.
Dissolving bits of rock, its tongue adheres
from birth to death, beneath the sun and moon.

It clings within the intertidal space,
enduring rhythmic pummels till submerged
for hours in liquid, when it scrapes its groove,
engulfing algae, seaweed in its wake.

An inch an hour is its pace beneath,
until the tide's reversed; it grips the granite
to endure another thrashing set, then rest
in radiant heat until the tide repeats.

What gives it strength to stay its radial path,
ripple its long foot and keep its grip—
hunger, fear of tumbling if unhinged,
a purpose to dissolve stone edge to sand?

How can one match the limpet's trek and rest
through ebb and flow of tide, in gales and floods,
in frost and sizzling heat upon its shell?
Exposed, its tendrils grip…and it persists.

Birch, Ice, Snow

Along the Merrimack

At dusk, along the river's edge
between the flow of tides,
the river glows in lavender
reflecting as it glides.

Ice floes pause along their trek;
herons land and play.
Birches stretched to touch the sky
(more camouflaged by day),

hint arabesque and some plié
above snow-covered ground—
they seem to twirl, leap in the air
to draw night's veil down.

Eagles nesting in red pines,
mallards by gold reeds,
bass below the fluid flow…
are still as light recedes.

Framed by shadows, white bark gleams,
branches arc and sway,
lit by dusk's reflected beams—
a moonlit birch ballet.

Float

Snowflakes float
as if in flight
in silence
as they spiral down—
crystals sparkling
day or night.
Snowflakes float
as if in flight
creating images
in white
as children sled
down hills in town.
Snowflakes float
as if in flight
in silence
as they spiral down.

Work or Play

What draws me to the soil in May?
When jonquils' yellow trumpets fade,
I wear loose clothes to dig all day.
I could be sipping lemonade.

Instead, I shape the yews with shears,
wear visored cap and cotton socks,
mix compost, loam, and sweat salt tears.
I tear through roots and toss small rocks.

I choose my plants for shade or sun;
form tiers; mix textures, spans of bloom;
plant periwinkles just for fun—
French marigolds, where I find room.

Memorial Day, my view, once plain,
is crowned by rainbows after rain.

Mother's Day

2016

The center of your universe? Not there.
Find just a tiny moon, reflecting light—
though sometimes barely visible, she's near.

You're the center of her orbit—dear
to her, her presence spinning day and night.
The center of the universe? Not there.

Lead your gaze beyond the clouds to where
the day or dark expanse of starlit night
reveals her, barely visible, but near.

She celebrates your birthdays every year;
she sees you change your world's course—her delight.
The center of the universe? Not there.

When meteors approach, she orbits near,
deflecting dust and particles—her light,
though sometimes barely visible, is near.

While traveling on your destined path, don't fear
her waxing, waning, fading from your sight.
The center of the universe? Not there.
Though barely visible at times, she's near.

She Dreamed

I'll be just fine when I can be
away from throbs you force on me;
away from light you use to burn
into my eyes, my brain, in turn;

away from rooms you spin around
and use to tilt me toward the ground;
away from new rugs, perfumed stores;
from champagne toasts and partiers;

away from music you instead,
reverberate inside my head;
away from dream-sleep you invade—
replace with thunder, lightning blades.

How I try to cap your hours,
but tears or fears recharge your powers.
I stay as calm as I can be,
imagine flowing rhythmically

in liquid, moving without haste
or sound or light or smell or taste—
so briefly, I escape your wrath
until you strike another path.

When you can't seize me, I enjoy
such rich hours you can't destroy.
This daily slog with you has been
so long but, Migraine, soon I'll win.

Mariposa Monarca

Monarch Butterfly

In waves of orange, sable, millions lift,
take flight aloft beside the ocean's mouth,
undulating high—the swell, a gift
above Quebec, Cape Cod, Cape May, and south.
Then west—they feed and mount a Gulf coast run.
Their fragile wings glide high on thermal air.
The earth's magnetic pull, the setting sun
guide the Monarchs' wings, and if they fare,
above the plains to mountain crests, in whirs
around, atop, warm giant oyamel firs.
By *Dia de los Muertos*, Day of the Dead,
they fold their tired wings—in prayer it's said—
then fall to sleep. Weighed branches bend, some break,
from clustered clumps the *Mariposas* make.

Come March, the *Mariposas* stir awake
atop Sierra Cinque's soaring peak—
a climb true lepidoptera lovers make
to see one hundred million wing pairs beat
above—aim north. They mimic light spring rain.
Their silhouetted bodies float and fade—
mate in Texas—then cross wide terrain,
lay eggs on milkweed under-leaves. Sparse shade
and dwindling fields greet more new wings in flight
toward eastern coasts, that after miles, alight
on milkweed leaves. Eggs hatch. More larvae feast,
and morph to wings that finally reach northeast.
Yet—females must lay hundreds, one by one,
or *this* Monarca odyssey's…undone.

Plunge

Raindrops plunge
through glistening air;
in streaks of mist,
they soak the ground
creating cloaks
of haze and glare.
Raindrops plunge
through glistening air
as tulips break
through soil once bare,
and children's boots
splash puddled ground.
Raindrops plunge
through glistening air;
in streaks of mist,
they soak the ground.

She Had To

With yet no place to go, she had to leave,
her belly swollen even rounder now.
In silence, knowing he would still deceive,
with yet no place to go, she had to leave.
Her mother hugged her, cried. She felt like Eve.
Her step-father's lust forced her to vow,
though yet no place to go, she had to leave,
her belly swollen even rounder now.

Solace

For Stephanie

"She has Trisomy 18,"
your obstetrician says.
"Presentation varies.
It is hard to predict."
He recommends abortion,
but gives you time to think.

You both say *yes* to Sophie,
share her every move
as she grows and fills your womb.
You feel her wonder, kicks—
sense her fingers grasp,
her tiny heart beat.

Cardinals fly about you—
trill, alight, build nests—
as if they are aware,
though some of Sophie's cells
cannot divide, she's one
of your dear family.

Sophie is your daughter.
Every day of her life
you sense your shared desires—
you listen to Brahms as one,
sing favorite lullabies,
coo lyric nursery rhymes.

She turns. She kicks. Her heart
beats for months inside
until the moment she
arrives, lips pursed, born…still.
Caressed and dressed in white,
she's ever in your arms.

Beneath His Bed

Beneath his bed, he hid from smoke and flame.
Only six, he gripped his toy and prayed,
wondering if his brothers were afraid.
So hard to breathe, this couldn't be a game.

The yellow crackling heat—if he could tame
its smoke, its creep beyond his door. It made
him cough. He hid his mouth to breathe. He'd trade
his favorite truck for help to cross that flame.

Tears ran down his cheeks. The window cracked.
Glass flew against the wall, the floor. The wild
flame caught his clothes, his hair. He couldn't see
the huge man sweep him up, but felt this act
was magic, heard the whisper, "Listen, child.
Don't be afraid. The fire won't follow me."

From Rubble

Six years old, awake, beneath his bed—
a fireman coaxed him, carried him away.

A helicopter whirled this helpless boy
away from melted toys and smoldering bed.
Alone, now safe, a thousand miles away—
inside a husk of acrid, scorched-black skin;
lost hair, lost nose, lost ears, lost fingers, toes;
corneas scarred; his eyelids barely closed—
skilled doctors patched on artificial skin.
He'll need so much more for years on end.

He holds his stuffed bear in his arm. His eyes
can't see how others see him now. He knows
he's strong enough to go. He's beat the odds
so far and needs a home outside these walls.
As tulips break through hard, but rain-soaked soil,
he must venture past protective doors.

In Olneyville

She was the first one who was wed.
Her mother showed no fear, no dread.
Her father did not speak a word—
for, against, she never heard.

The outdoor setting by the tower—
the cake, the band, and every flower,
the meal—was in the end, agreed
upon by bride and groom. The need

for life insurance cash bared more,
her uncle's comment by the door—
"You can't marry everyone
you love." No explanation. None.

In gown and veil with lace and pearl,
she watched her groom's dark side unfurl.

Shimmer

Sun rays shimmer
in the air.
Time melts as foam-
topped waves crash down
on sparkling sand
out by the pier.
Sun rays shimmer
in the air.
At high tide,
castles disappear.
A child's towel
becomes a gown.
Sun rays shimmer
in the air.
Time melts as foam-
topped waves crash down.

Ribbons, Buttons, Lace

The last time mother closed her sewing machine,
she'd sewn my sister's gown of silk and lace,
a veil with pearls, fulfilling her own wish.
The house, now her own space, would have no hum.
She'd reached the private goal she'd set herself:
to dress each daughter till her wedding day...

plus bridesmaids' gowns and her own dress that day.
She'd learned how fabrics stressed her one machine
and oiled it well; used threads she chose herself.
She learned the slip of silk, the weave of lace,
required she guide her Singer, feel its hum—
with yards and yards of fabric toward her wish

of daughters dressed by her—beyond her wish
when she took *her* vows on her wedding day.
While her love served in Normandy, she'd hum
soft tunes of his return—no sewing machine.
Her trousseau was of borrowed silk and lace.
Her groom gave her a "Singer." She'd teach herself.

She made her first dress simply, for herself—
an A-line shift in navy blue. Her wish
for Christmas velvet, Easter's hand-made lace,
came first in trimmings for the holiday.
When babies came, she cherished her machine;
her babies breathed in rhythm with its hum.

She'd set the bobbin, press the footplate, hum
a favorite tune, and fit each dress herself
in pastels, flowered prints, as her machine
sewed ribbons, pleats—yes, every daughter's wish
for birthdays, dances, gowns for Spring prom day—
velvet, chiffon, rayon, linen, lace.

All sewing done, she stored away her lace...
knit blankets, scarves, a while...soon wonder, hums—
lost words from lullabies. On shopping days
with daughters, friends, she lost her sense of self,
what was said and where she was—her wish
undone, instead confusion: what machine,

what meal, what day, what daughter, what saved lace?
Old photos proved how her machine *did* hum.
Our wish? Her awe: "I stitched each dress...myself?"

Rushmore

My father dreamed his carving skill
would never leave his hand. He still
might shape his final block of wood:
determined to, as best he could,
hew icons, four, by force of will—

beyond his eagle, whippoorwill,
his bluejay on my windowsill.
Dementia threatened: *how* he would,
my father dreamed.

Though progress day-by-day was nil,
in months, a nose, a mouth showed skill.
Soon Lincoln's features formed the wood.
As sawdust fell, Dad understood
his mind's decline, but with his drill,
my father dreamed.

Hours Arrested

After Six Months

Again, Mom turns Dad's band on her right hand
and eyes the one with whom she shares the room.
Mom whispers, frowns, "But I don't understand.

How long has Dad been gone?" Her day's unplanned.
He'd be beside her, carving—memories loom
again. She turns his band on her right hand.

"Did I go to his wake?" Can she withstand
repeated jolts? She broods, "He was my groom,"
then whispers, frowns, "But I don't understand."

She nods, "I moved here once I lost him," and
her loss of time, his absence, fill the room.
She turns Dad's wedding band on her right hand

and glances at Dad's photos on the stand
beside her, near the jasmine lush with bloom.
She whispers, frowns, "But I don't understand."

The valentine she made for him by hand
fades on her memo board. The man for whom
she turns the band again on her right hand
is gone. She frowns, "But I don't understand."

Lift

Leaves lift free
on chilling gusts
and rustle, whisper,
swirl around—
orange, yellow,
red, then rust.
Leaves lift free
on chilling gusts
while children trick
or treat with trust
and scarecrows, pumpkins
dot the ground.
Leaves lift free
on chilling gusts
and rustle, whisper,
swirl around.

Paulette Demers Turco is a member of Alfred Nicol's biweekly poetry workshop and Rhina Espaillat's annual Lyceum workshop, both in Newburyport, MA. She has attended the annual Robert Frost Farm poetry conferences since the first in 2015.

Her poems are published in *The Lyric; Ibbetson Street Press; Merrimac Mic Anthology II: Going with the Floes,* 2016; (poems and art) *Merrimac Mic Anthology III: The River Widens,* 2017, and *Merrimac Mic Anthology IV: watershed,* 2018, anthologies edited by Isabell VanMerlin. *In Silence* is her first chapbook. Presently a student at Lesley University MFA in Writing Poetry program in Cambridge, MA, she has been awarded the Lesley University MFA in Writing Presidential Scholarship. Her poem, *The Limpet*, won honorable mention in the 2014 Naomi Cherkofsky Memorial North Shore Poetry contest.

She participates in open mics sponsored by the Powow River Poets in Newburyport, MA; Portsmouth, NH Poet Laureate Poetry Hoot; Newburyport's Joppa Flats, Art and the Experience of Nature; Amesbury Library Poet Laureate Program, and Merrimac Mic in Merrimac, MA.

Growing up in Rhode Island, she learned to knit, crochet, sew, and do other crafts that now weave their way into her poems. She is a semi-retired optometrist in a large sub-specialty eye-care practice on the North Shore. She lives in Newburyport, MA where she enjoys being near family, travel, drawing, acrylic painting and writing for young people.

www.ingramcontent.com/pod-product-compliance
Lightning Source LLC
LaVergne TN
LVHW041522070426
835507LV00012B/1751